with being a nurse or a farmer or a dentist or a teacher? Then sometimes I think about those people who are, not nurses and doctors, but who, you know, appear to live, as it were, a very simple life, but who actually have fantastic influence, and make a real difference to their community. And they're the perfect example of how God doesn't value one person over another because of what they do. It's just because you exist, you matter.

JIM: I think I have done that at times, and particularly in my youth, when worshipping at the local parish church where I was brought up in Glasgow, it seemed to me that other young people carried evidence of their faith and commitment in the form of their crucifixes around their necks or other signs. I did feel feelings of inadequacy as far as my value in God's eyes. I think my confidence grew with exposure to a bit more learning about New Testament teaching and what was expected of people, and the assurance that the outward signs weren't the important ones.

FRANCES: I haven't felt as though I was less important to God than other people. But I have felt that other people have felt that I was less important than other people.

Well, they're all a bit unsure of their value and with feelings of inadequacy. Do you think that's common among believers, Carmody?

CG: Yes, I think that's extremely common. In fact, I might even say it's almost universal. And I think it's very important to acknowledge, and to be willing to say that in front of ourselves and others – that we do struggle with feelings of inadequacy, and that being a Christian doesn't, as it were, save us from that, in any straightforward sense. It doesn't take away our insecurities overnight. It doesn't suddenly transform us into people who need nothing and are afraid of nothing. The gospel addresses us in exactly that place, the place of our insecurity and our fear and our weakness. And it's an ultimate reassurance that God values us. In the company of Jesus we don't need to see that others are somehow less good, in order to feel more good ourselves. In the world of the gospel, God's affirmation of me and God's affirmation of you, come together, and so God, as it were, heals us in our insecure places together with others, and not apart from them.

[3]

Thank you. Now I believe you were brought up in a non-religious family, but when were thirteen, you got a shock when you wandered into your local parish church for the first time. Could you tell us the story briefly?

CG: I went to a very secular school, where I wasn't actually allowed to go to church. There was no chapel or church on the school grounds and there was no religious education. There was no chaplain. There were no prayers. There were no hymns. There was nothing in my education that gave me a sort of sense of what Christianity was about. I eventually took it on myself to wander down to our local village, to be able to get into our parish church, and I think it is one of the most extraordinary turning points of my whole life. The church was just like a foreign world, and it was in that context that I found myself walking around the church, and reading the messages in the stained glass windows, and finding it unutterably strange. And then the strangest thing of all was my encounter with this image of Saint Peter, who was holding a banner in the window and I was standing there for a long time, trying to make out what the words said, and finally realizing that what they said was: 'For behold, I perceive that God is no respecter of persons', and I was absolutely baffled. The church was completely empty. I stood there for a long time by myself thinking, 'Wow, these people worship a God who doesn't respect any one', [*laughs*] and it made a very deep impression on me and at first, of course I was disturbed. And then, as I went away and reflected, and processed, and looked it up in a modern Bible – and I realized that this wasn't about God not respecting people in general, it was about God not taking people's status – social status – into account, in the way he related to them. Christianity was not a religion in which God took notice of people's social status. That was the first thing I knew about Christians – that was really their trademark for me from then on.

I asked our Voices if they ever find it difficult to understand things in the Bible that seem contrary to what they thought the Bible says. And if so, how did they get to see another way of interpreting the Bible?

BERNADETTE: I think that happens all the time. We often misunderstand what we read because it's not written for our culture, it's not written for our own time, so we have to try and understand what it meant at the time, where it was coming from, what it was trying to achieve. And that's why we need good teachers. We need good interpreters to help us to do that. You can't expect everybody to spend their lives studying theology. But at the same time I think we also — we need perhaps to listen to the Spirit, because there's so much of our life that simply isn't described in the Bible. It's a constant learning process. It's never quite what it looks like, is it.

FRANCES: I sometimes find it difficult to understand things in the Bible the way my husband understands things in the Bible, and I sometimes see them contrary to what might have been said. I'm on a journey with discovering how things are said.

JIM: Yes I do find a good deal of it difficult to truly understand. What should I do in response to what I am reading or hearing here? A lot of biblical and church talk is in metaphor and sometimes the significance or the comparison isn't clearly evident to me. I think that reading and hearing, preaching and following up in other secular reading and so on provokes me to think a good deal more, and to jump to conclusions a little bit less. How do I get to see another way of interpreting things that I've read in the Bible? I continue to think and reflect — sometimes to no adequate conclusion.

[4]
So, Carmody, do you find the Bible a constant learning process? Or is it just unreliable?

CG: I had — and have — an unusual relationship with it, in the sense that I never got used to it. It never sounded just familiar and obvious to me. Every part of it sounded strange, unexpected, difficult, sort of bumpy. You know, the experience of reading the Bible for me — which I did completely by myself as a teenager — was bumpy. I thought we shouldn't too quickly try to familiarize or domesticate the Bible, we actually need to make efforts to *unfamiliarize* ourselves with it, to *undomesticate* it, to let it speak to us again with its great strangeness, because it's a story. The Bible, as a whole, is a story of humanity coming to learn and understand and know things about itself, you know, the ultimate image of this for me is Jacob wrestling with the angel. It's a wrestling. The Bible is something that we wrestle with throughout our life, and it's not a problem if we are wrestling with it. I would say it's a problem if we *aren't* wrestling with it.

[5]

Let's just go to Jesus for a moment or two, and one of his parables – sheep and goats – and it teaches that whatever we do to any human, good or bad, we do to him. That's from Matthew 25:40. So how do you think it's possible to treat everyone we know – or don't know – as though they were Christ? I think that's quite difficult. Anyway, Bernadette kicks off again.

BERNADETTE: I have no idea [*laughing*]. It's impossible isn't it – it is actually impossible. You'd have to think actively, all of the time, this person is as Christ to me, and you'd constantly be doing a kind of double-think, and yet, and yet – that is sort of what's asked of us. We're just asked to do our best, aren't we – isn't that what that means?

JIM: I think this is a teaching in a number of the mainstream religions besides Christianity, that we should treat others as we would wish to be treated. The 'golden rule'. And perhaps that at its basis is how to go about treating everyone – whether we know them or don't know them – as though they were Christ. To treat them as we would wish to be treated.

FRANCES: I spent some time in my life with the Quakers, listening, waiting, and there was a lovely thing that George Fox said about the light of God in every man or woman. And I think if we can see the image of God in everybody, then we can love everybody. Being able to see that we're all created in the image of God is a way in which we can treat everyone we know, or don't know, as though they were Christ.

Okay, so what do you think of those?

CG: Of course, in one sense, it is impossible, and I think it's important to be up front about the scale of, as it were, of perfection that we're being invited to strive for in this parable. But I don't think that that's a reason for despair, as it were. I don't think it's a reason to view it as something impossible to achieve. It's about seeing this passage in the context of the whole message of Jesus, which is that Christ and the Spirit do in us what we're not capable of doing. That it's not about just relying on my own efforts at any point. It's not about *me* having to be a moral hero and climb the mountain of moral perfection – you know, with my own bare strength. That's not the overall message of the gospel, and of the Bible, and by the way this touches on the point about the Bible that we always need to pay attention to the whole story. We need to let every individual episode and every individual teaching be seen in the perspective of the whole story. And the whole story is a story of God, saying: This is what a flourishing human life looks like. It looks like a life in which we treat all people as though they were the image of God, which is Christ, but that that life isn't something that you live by yourself. It's not something that you achieve just by waking up in the morning and deciding to do it. It's something you grow into by being in the company of Jesus, and that Jesus walks with you. The destination is encountering every person as Christ. I just want to say one other thing about this as well, in relation to, particularly what Bernadette said. I don't think that what we're being asked to do is have a completely conscious, explicit thought all the time: 'This person is Christ. This person is Christ. This person is Christ.' That would just be an exhausting way to live, and not really helpful either. I don't think it's about what's going on consciously, so it doesn't have to be always that conscious explicit thought. It's more like over time, by practice, I become somebody who is capable of always treating people as though they were Jesus – whether I'm thinking about it or not. And thinking about it at that level of habit, rather than at the level of this kind of massive effort of moral will all the time is a much healthier and more a human way to think about it, I think.

Thank you. Now we're going to move to Session Two.

[6]
SESSION 2
NEITHER JEW NOR GENTILE

Carmody, you were brought up in a very liberal home where you and your siblings were free to express yourselves, and so on. There were very few rules – but just one, that was sacrosanct. 'Leave no one out.' Tell us about that and the importance of it on your life.

CG: It's no exaggeration to say that it's been the moral standard, the moral inspiration, the challenge of my whole life. And to this day I would say that it's the keynote of Christianity. Absolutely every person is sanctified in Christ. When God becomes human in Christ, he changes and touches and enters into the depths of the life of every single human being. And when I discovered that about Christ – about Christianity – I realized that, whether it was difficult or not, that I would try to live like that.

Thank you. Thank you. That's lovely. I wondered if our Voices could identify with this urge to club together with like-minded people.

JIM: My own family were more prescriptive. I grew up with some pretty firm rules in the household about conduct and expectations, but among those rules there was always encouragement to be inclusive, not to ignore the other child who wasn't joining in the activity. As I reached thirteen years of age and was associated at school and in uniformed organizations, with groups within those groups – but that in itself meant we were a group that was excluding others who didn't wear those uniforms, or participate in those activities. And unconsciously doing so. So it's a matter, I think, about becoming aware that just joining together still tends to be exclusive.

BERNADETTE: My childhood home was very open. It was multi-ethnic, multi-cultural, multi-religion, multi-faith – as well as whatever bits of Christianity crept into there as well. 'Everybody welcome, take care of everybody' kind of household. But school was very different. Probably because I grew up in that kind of household that was like nobody else's home – so I didn't belong at school. I felt very outside of the groups at school, until I began to find something of a personal faith, and there were one or two other young people like me, but then of course we became very clubabble and I didn't really like that. I didn't really want to belong in that kind of way.

FRANCES: So I remember when my dad went to the local shop for a newspaper. And he came back with a Spanish student! And this Spanish student had been putting up in the newsagent's a postcard saying he needed a place to stay, and my dad saw this postcard, and said, 'Well, why don't you stay with us?' So he had gone for a newspaper, but he came back with a Spanish student, and I think he stayed with us for about four months. I don't know if it was because my dad was the son of a vicar in Ghana – so it was a case of the vicarage was always open. My origins are from Ghana and 'Akwaaba' is what you see when you come into the airport – Accra airport, when you come in, it says in big letters: 'Akwaaba' and 'Akwaaba' means 'welcome'. I love that scripture which talks about how you never know who you're letting in – it could be an angel, so it's important to be kind to others.

[7]
This exclusivity can be a danger for the Church, and Paul recognized this right from the earliest days of Christianity. In Galatians he notes that the Christians in Galatia, having heard and accepted the good news that God loves them, might well become a new exclusive club. He emphasizes that, by definition, the Christian faith is totally inclusive: 'There is no longer Jew or Gentile, no longer slave or free, no longer male or female, for all of you are one in Christ Jesus.' Carmody, how well in your experience does today's Church follow that rule of 'leaving no-one out'?

CG: I think we should be very careful about criticizing the Church as though from outside of it, and I'll explain what I mean here. There's a wonderful Catholic author of the mid-twentieth century – a monk and a hermit and a follower of the great apostle to Africa, Charles de Foucauld. He's called Carlo Carretto, and he wrote about what's going on when we say that we don't want to be part of the Church, or that we hate the Church or that the Church is a failure. That often what's operating is a secret expectation that the church will be somehow different from what we are. Whereas in fact, the Church just is us, projected onto a large screen. All my own failures and all my own weaknesses, as well as all of my own gifts and potentials are there in the Church, just as they are in me. And what we shouldn't do is unrealistically expect that the Church will be are different from myself. There's no magic pill that means that when Christians get together, somehow their weaknesses and their failures disappear. Any more than when I get together with others, my weaknesses and failures disappear. And that's not supposed – that's not intended in any way to be a licence for churches to fail, but it does mean that when churches leave others out, which they routinely do of course, the question we should ask is not: 'How on earth could this happen?' but: 'Where am I doing this in my life? And how can I witness to a better and truer picture of the Church as myself?' And to just be a little bit careful about the tendency to always say that it's the fault of the Church.

[8]

Yes, that's very interesting. I'd like to just go a bit deeper into that, if we can, because I think in a sense what you said, I feel, well, that's easy to say, because, you know, that isn't the way that other people outside the Church often see the Church. And as you say, those of us in the Church don't often see it like that, so I just wondered if our Voices are of the same mind as you. How well in their experience does today's Church follow the rule of 'leaving no one out'?

BERNADETTE: Oh, the Church is hopeless. But then the Church is made up of people – we're people, and we leave people out all of the time. We might not mean to sometimes – we do it by mistake – and sometimes it is done deliberately. So you get your middle-class church where other people might feel they wouldn't be welcome, even though they might be, but others might not know how to make them welcome. We're just hopeless at it.

FRANCES: Well I think, sadly, it doesn't follow that rule. I remember at drama school my vocal coach saying to me, 'Frances, you see things with rose-tinted glasses, this isn't the way the world is really,' but I think in my rose-tinted glasses I would have liked to believe that that wouldn't have existed in the Church, in terms of the exclusivity, racism, the -isms, but sadly it does exist. It does exist. And it is an issue that needs to be addressed. What are we going to do about it? How are we going to – because we are called to do the right thing.

JIM: Sadly, I don't think the Church achieves the rule of leaving no one out. I think that the members of the various denominations tend to wish not to leave anyone out, but there is, unwittingly, a feeling that *our* denomination and the way we worship and the way we practise, and the things we do to support society and support our mission, and support charitable organizations, is the right way. And that's pretty dangerous.

CG: Yes, so I think that Bernadette and Frances and Jim are absolutely correct that the Church fails in that regard – routinely. But it's very easy to also not see the ways in which the Church also succeeds. The fact that half of all health care in Africa is provided by Christian churches, completely for free, is never mentioned. And that's not in any way supposed to be a licence for Christian failure. We have a tendency to pick out the failures. It is entirely the case that every church community is littered with examples of people who don't feel welcome for one reason or another – and there are different types of people in different churches, right. This is another important thing to recognize. The question is: Let's not expect the Church to be a collection of superheroes, because I am not a superhero. The people in the pew next to me are not superheroes. What we are, is people who are relying on the grace of God, to grow slowly over time into being better versions of ourselves.

[9]
I think, let's just go a little bit broader. There are plenty of categories within religion – often opposed categories: secularists versus religious, atheists versus believers, Christians versus Muslims, Catholics versus Protestants, and so on. Is it ever going to be possible to reconcile these differences? Our Voices are tentative, I have to say.

FRANCES: It depends on how much people are willing to be honest and open. I think if people are willing to talk and engage, then it will be possible to reconcile these differences. So it's a case of, even though it may be awkward or difficult, people need to have conversations. And when people are willing to be open, and to talk, that's where change can happen.

BERNADETTE: Well we do tend to take up positions. So I do think personal encounter, working together on things, building things together, building society together – and real relationship, that's probably *the* only way that could ever be overcome.

JIM: If we interpret 'reconcile' as meaning 'to restore friendly relations' I am fairly confident we are moving towards it. There are less entrenched views being uttered in the upper and administrative reaches of the church groups, and multi-faith groups too. So reconciliation to that extent I think is gradually taking place. Is it ever going to be possible to reconcile them, in the sense that we will all pull together confidently? I can offer you no confident assurance on that.

CG: I think Bernadette and Frances are completely right that reconciliation, concretely speaking, absolutely depends on a willingness to never give up on that process of personal encounter, to quote Bernadette, of 'working together on things, building things together, building society together and building real relationships'. That's what reconciliation is. It doesn't happen in a kind of abstract space. It happens in our commitment to actually building relationships with people, with whom we differ day by day by day by day. It doesn't – you know, it's not just a nice idea, it's the concrete reality of loving people, walking with people, being in communion with people, sharing common projects with people. And if reconciliation is going to happen, it's going to happen like that. And as Frances says, it is often awkward and difficult. And by the way, I think that a really good image from popular culture of what reconciliation looks like – a kind of non-romantic picture of reconciliation – is in the film which I recommend anybody to watch – although maybe with a blindfold for some parts of it. It's called *Five Minutes of Heaven*. *Five Minutes of Heaven* is about reconciliation in the context of the conflict in Northern Ireland, and what we see in that film is that reconciliation is not a romantic dream. It's not pretty. It's not fluffy. It's the very, very gritty, constantly challenging process of loving another person just as they are, in that place that they're in. In terms of Jim's comments, what exactly does 'reconciliation' mean? Does it mean to restore friendly relations, or does it mean something more than that? I think being a Christian means, among other things, believing God's promise for human beings that we will be reconciled. That in some way we are already reconciled in Christ – you know, to quote the scripture, 'we are all one in Christ Jesus'. Christ is already the present reality of our reconciliation. Living with Christ means living out of that truth. Differences are not alternatives. We don't have to choose between male or female, Jew or Gentile. It's a reconciliation that is deeper than any of these identities, and Christians are called to live that truth, even in a world where reconciliation is still, in so many cases a distant dream. And churches, of course, are ideally places where we see that reconciliation taking place. But the very short answer to the question: 'Reconciliation – ever or never?' the very short answer is: 'Always.' Christian life is *always* about reconciliation. There's never, ever a resting point where we can say we've done enough.

Thank you so much. We're going to move to another contentious subject in Session Three.

SESSION 3
NEITHER MALE NOR FEMALE

Carmody, you were told off when you used the word 'mankind' instead of 'humanity' in your essays at university. Why do you think it worried them so much?

CG: I think it worried them because maleness is considered normative or standard humanity, and femaleness is considered a deviation from that. You know, the human, the kind of ideal human, or the archetype of the human, is taken to be male, and females are just a sort of less good, or slightly broken or second-rate version of the ideal humanity. And of course that has its roots at least as far back as Aristotle, and is slightly expressed in our language, in the difference between female and male. That female is just kind of male, with a bit added on. And when we talk about *all* human beings with the word 'mankind', or just 'man', we're really reproducing and embedding that understanding. Even if we don't think about it. Even if we aren't conscious of it. That's why I was pulled up on it at university. Because as long as we refer to the whole human race with a word that also refers to maleness, then at some level in our consciousness we reinforcing the idea that maleness is the standard humanity, and that females are a deviation from that. So that's what I think the worry is.

What do our Voices think? 'Mankind' or 'humanity'? Which do they prefer?

BERNADETTE: Oh I think Carmody was rightly told off! 'Male and female they were created,' so the text goes. I think we're not 'mankind', we're human beings all together, we're men and women and all points in between. And 'mankind' is a very curious word. And I think an unhelpful one actually, today, to try and describe what it is to be human. So I would prefer 'humanity'.

FRANCES: I think it's a bit dated and I think 'humanity' is something that I would prefer. I have a woman's Bible, and throughout it, whenever they say things like 'brothers' then they put 'and sisters' so it's the recognizing everybody. So I do prefer 'humanity'.

JIM: I side with Carmody. I think looking within the word 'humanity', 'man' appears, and 'mankind' describes us adequately. In my view it's perfectly reasonable to call our species 'mankind'.

[11]
So do you think they've grasped the point of the issue?

CG: I think – I say this tentatively and respectfully – that the issue is actually extremely serious about the language that we use. I'm not sure that it's just to do with things being dated. And I'm of a mind to think that Bernadette is on to it when she says I was rightly told off. But I would want to put it more strongly than her when she says she thinks it's an unhelpful term. I think it's more than unhelpful. I think it's very damaging, at a level that we aren't even conscious of, that the language that we use really reinforces a certain perception of reality, and we do need to be alert to that. But I think we shouldn't be naive either about the significance of our vocabulary. And we see that in all kinds of ways, in different aspects of our language. But this is a particularly obvious way in which we can innocently as in, without even realizing it, reinforce the perception that males come first and females are a sort of after-thought, in relation to human nature.

But what about Jim's point, which he says, 'humanity' has got 'man' in the middle of it?

CG: Yes, but I think it's not, it's not insignificant that the word 'man' refers to human males. That's the issue. The word 'woman' doesn't appear, but the word 'man' does, but I don't think that the fact that the word 'man' appears in the word 'humanity' is enough to justify using 'mankind', because a woman is a human, but a woman is not a man. If we could have a new word, I would vote for a new word, but I'm not sure that language works like that. [*Laughs.*] Maybe 'people'.

[12]
You write: 'For most women in our world, being female is still a terrible disadvantage. Across huge swathes of our globe you are still likely to

*thank God for being born a male and lament being born female.' Is
there any way of changing this way of thinking, or is the world stuck with
it? We're going to hear the Voices again and then see how you respond
to that.*

BERNADETTE: Well, we can't afford to be stuck with it. But I had
an example only last night, as I walked with my daughter and
tiny new-born granddaughter to the lift of her building where
she lives, and a man stopped her and said, 'New baby?' and
she said, 'Yes!' He said, 'Boy?' and she said, 'No' and he said,
'Huh!' and walked on. His wife followed swiftly behind and the
conversation was repeated exactly. So this is very, very deep
in some cultures and has a long, long way to go. It is changing
and I think particularly in the West where we are engaging
much more with issues of gender as opposed to simply talking
about biological sex and therefore we're beginning to recognize
increasingly that the business of being male or female is not
necessarily the most helpful way to talk about these issues, but
it is difficult for women constantly to fight for their place and it's
exhausting actually. I think I would say it has been very tiring as a
woman at times to fight for my place, to fight for equal pay, to go
to the boss and say, 'You're paying someone who's doing exactly
the same job as me for more money. Can you explain why? I
would like the same.' One shouldn't have to do that. It's a long,
long journey. And in the West we are beginning to talk about this
easily – much more easily. I think for some other cultures it's an
incredibly difficult journey.

FRANCES: Again I think it's through open discussion about things.
For example, if I think about myself and in my marriage with
my husband, women are – we're not equals. We're not seen as
equals. You know, at the end of the day he leads, and what he
says goes, and it's a constant discussion that we have. And I think
it's not something that you're just stuck with – it is changing. It is
changing, which is positive. It is positive.

JIM: In my lifetime I've seen gradual change towards more
inclusivity, more equality, but it's very slow and gradual, and
it's pretty much confined to liberal Western democracies and
even there it's pretty patchy. Is there any way of changing this

way of thinking? Only by example. Only by showing how those liberal Western democracies which have adopted equality have improved in terms of relationships and less violence and more productivity and more care. Only by example.

Gradual change. Is that enough?

CG: It's not enough. It's not enough, but we need to balance the sense of urgency and impatience with a sense of pragmatic engagement with the concrete circumstances we're in which always resist and push back change. I think we should be impatient. Women around the world suffer indescribably, because we haven't been impatient enough, and we still routinely underestimate the extraordinary costs of being female in most societies today. So no, gradual change is not enough, and we should be impatient, and there is no such thing as too urgent, when it comes to the liberation of women from misogyny. But, we work with what we have.

I asked the Voices if they could see any reason why the male/female divide should be allowed to continue or be sustained in any aspect of Christian life, given that in Christ there is no longer any male or female and that all are one in Jesus Christ. Here's what they said.

BERNADETTE: Well, clearly it doesn't mean that there isn't male and there isn't female, it means that those things are not important in Christ. We are people – that's what we are. We are all people. And we all need to be loved and respected and cared for and cherished. And it doesn't matter who you are, whether you're male, female and all points in-between, we're just people.

FRANCES: I think we should celebrate males, and we should celebrate females, and I think we're in a bit of a tricky place at the moment, if I'm honest. I do. I think we are all 'fearfully and wonderfully made'.

JIM: I can be quite brief in answer to this: I see no reason at all why the male/female divide should be permitted to continue for a moment longer in church.

[13]
And you, Carmody, should the Church ever favour either men or women?

CG: The Church should always be a witness to the reality of what is proclaimed in that message from Paul, that in Christ there is no male or female. We should always ask, and expect, and look for the Church to represent that. But I don't think we need to be aiming for a church in which there is no such thing as sex difference, or there is no such thing as gender difference. But when it comes to favouring – absolutely not. Absolutely not.

You write that having seen Christ, having known and encountered Christ, the authors of the New Testament find themselves having to rethink the concepts and the framework that they had received from the past, whether Jewish or Greek. Has your encounter with Christ changed the way you think about things?

CG: There's nothing, anywhere in my life, that hasn't been changed by that encounter. And by the way I don't mean that therefore I'm living a transformed life. I don't mean changed in the right way, or in an adequate way, but simply in the sense of the challenge. It's a total challenge. It's a total invitation. It's a total reorientation. I would say that – even though I wouldn't for a moment dare to think that my life had been changed in the right ways or in enough ways – that it has been changed completely. And that includes my thinking. It's the base challenge of my life, really. And I react differently to that challenge every day. Very often I will push it away. Very often I will refuse it, but its impact is all-pervasive.

Thank you very much for that honesty. Now Session Four awaits.

[14]
SESSION 4
NEITHER SLAVE NOR FREE

Carmody, your father was a photojournalist and you travelled with him around the world from a very early age. And you encountered the slavery of extreme poverty. Can you tell us what it did to you – how you coped seeing such awful things?

CG: I'm not sure that I did cope. I recall extreme distress. It left me with something like a constant unease. When I sort of encountered Christianity, I found a way of living with that unease, which was at the same time an invitation to never walk away from it. And Christianity represented both of those to me – both a way of having some kind of peace in the light of the things that I had seen, at the same time as having an absolute mandate not to avoid those realities.

What, as Christians or as the Church, can we actually do about such situations? I know it's a massive thing to answer – a massive question really. I did ask the Voices what they had to say about it.

FRANCES: I think of that saying about evil exists when good people do nothing, so I think if it's in your capability to do something, then we can make changes. So, it's seeing and doing.

BERNADETTE: I think one has to start with prayer – about oneself, prayer about the situation, and reflection, before doing anything. Because rushing into doing isn't necessarily very helpful. There is a lot to do and I think some have the capacity and a sense of calling to really be in those situations to make a physical difference, personally by being there. I think others are able to play their part in campaigning, bringing those things to wider audience, to greater attention, to helping people to engage. Others, if you have money, you can give money. If you don't have either that sense of calling, or you feel you don't have the courage to do, there is always *something* at some level one can do. And there is prayer. But it's never enough. Whatever we do is *never* enough. There is always more that can be done. And it is an unending challenge.

JIM: I think we must consider very carefully almost everything that we do. You know, manufacturing having moved offshore, we reap the benefits of inexpensive goods and services and food and so on, and as we speak, those chickens are coming home to roost, because of the world situation, post-Covid. We need to think very, very hard about the cheap clothes that we buy. And just not be tempted to buy them – try to make things last longer. It's not just a matter I think of raising funds, and exporting the funds, and feeling good about it, and then buying cheap manufactured goods, ignoring the fact that maybe child labour or long hours – or any number of awful things happening to result in our cheap purchase. We need to discipline ourselves, and stop and think at every turn. We need to make charities accountable for expenditure.

[15]
Carmody, we have to try something surely. What do you suggest?

CG: What can I do? What am I called to do? What am I capable of doing? What am I gifted to do? What am I resourced to do? And we also ask those questions at the level of our local Christian community, at the level of our regional church, or our national Church or the global Church. Right. The questions are asked at every level and different things are possible. So, I like the fact that Jim mentions the role of, broadly speaking, consumer ethics. One thing that is extremely obvious to Christians in the developed West is that we have tremendous power as consumers. Taking responsibility for that power is one of the things that being Christian means for us, in this time, in this place. And that means, as Jim said, it means clothes. It means food. It means all kinds of manufactured goods. It means energy. It means holidays. It means, you know – I like to say as a kind of shorthand for this, that every time we spend our money, we are casting a vote for the kind of world we want. That's a fundamental form of taking Christian responsibility for Christians in the developed West, but it's not the fundamental form for Christians – many Christians – living in the global South, who have very little or no consumer power. So once again, it's contextual. But speaking to those who are in a social situation like ours, consumer power is an absolutely fundamental part of it – particularly in the context of climate change, environmental change. Taking responsibility for the way we spend our money as consumers is absolutely critical. Right – that's one thing we must do about it. The other thing is, I think we routinely underestimate our political power. We underestimate the fact that we live in a democracy. We have the opportunity to influence the decisions that are made. We have the opportunity to apply pressure on our leaders. We have the opportunity to indicate whether we accept, or don't accept, the decisions that they make on our behalf. We must act as consumers and as citizens in a democracy. But beyond that I think that the question we must ask is: 'What am I resourced and gifted to do?' Christian life doesn't look the same for everybody. Quite the opposite. Every single person imitates Christ, and is indwelled by the Spirit in a different way. And we take inspiration from what it looks like in other lives, but ultimately, we look at our own life, and we say: today, with this body, this mind, this heart, these relationships, these resources, these opportunities – what do I do?

[16]

Let's turn to the Church specifically. You write in the early Church, the issues of differences in status or importance was an issue. James, the leader of the first church in Jerusalem, wrote to the congregation: 'If a person with gold rings and in fine clothes comes into your assembly, and if a poor person in dirty clothes also comes in, and if you take notice of the one wearing the fine clothes and say, "Have a seat here, please," while to the other one who is poor you say, "Stand there," or, "Sit at my feet," have you not made distinctions amongst yourselves . . ? . . . Do you with your acts of favouritism really believe in our glorious Lord Jesus Christ?'

That's quite powerful I think, isn't it. I asked the Voices if they see such acts of favouritism or discrimination still present in the Church today.

BERNADETTE: Well of course they are. I hesitate to say this, but I might as well say it: why do we pay our clergy different amounts depending on the seniority of their role in the Church? You know, why does an Archbishop have to live where he has to live? Or a Bishop in a palace – or whatever? Why is that necessary? I know these are very small things, but they are a picture of the Church. This is what people look at. And it's not a picture of the Church leadership living among the people, living and serving among the people. And you might argue, 'Oh well, they need to get away because it's all exhausting.' Actually, a parish priest's work is *incredibly* exhausting, it's just of a different order. Well, that's just one example. Yes, of course the Church practises favouritism.

FRANCES: Yes I think so. I really like the book of James, and I was looking at that whole chapter not so long ago about impartiality, and so it is something that's very close to my heart. But I have seen it where people have gravitated to people who are wealthy, maybe encouraged them a little bit more, invited them over to dinner, they wanted them to stay in the presence in the church, and you have little social groups that start up, of like-minded people. I think it's that sense of 'What can they bring? What can they offer the church?' whereas somebody in dirty clothes, who is poor – what can they bring, but dependency? You know, having to give to them more.

JIM: I think it's true to say that the community where I regularly worship is highly educated, largely middle-class, comfortably-off to wealthy, and we seldom get visitors who are in the truly ragged, needy, drug-dependent or alcohol-dependent fringes of society. On the other hand, among our congregations there are those who make it their business to go to quite nearby communities and to care for homeless rough sleepers, hungry, needy in multiple ways, and that's an actual spin-off motivated by their faith and I hope reinforced by joining us in worship.

So what do you think about this, Carmody?

CG: I think I agree with all of our Voices. Of course, the Church practises favouritism. But to repeat something I said before, that's because *we* practise favouritism. The Church is just us. It's just us, projected onto a large screen. Yes, the Church practises favouritism and yes, we have never come to the end of the project of overcoming that. We have never come to the end of the project of trying to live up to the God who has no favourites.

Thank you. Yes, indeed.

[17]
Pope Francis talks about the 'peripheries', the edges of the world where so many people live. Not only the geographical edges of the world,

but also the social, economic and spiritual margins – the vast ranks of the excluded, those who have been left behind. Shut out. And it's there, on the peripheries, Jesus was to be found. He went on to be with the vast ranks of the excluded. And those who follow him are asked to go there, too. I asked the Voices how this made them feel: uncomfortable, ashamed, helpless, challenged? Or are they okay with that situation?

JIM: It does make me feel a bit uncomfortable. I think we're easily sold on the current slogan of 'levelling up'. And you know, that means we don't need to do anything to reduce our well-being and our comfortable status – and I feel challenged by it. I'm once again going to offer you no easy solution, but it's something I ponder on quite a lot.

BERNADETTE: I'm definitely challenged by it. The Church doesn't really belong in the centre. It belongs on the edge. It believes it should be in the centre and somehow relevant, but the Church isn't called to be relevant, it is called to be prophetic. And the prophets, although they entirely embrace their own culture, they don't sit in the middle of the culture, they sit on the edge, where they can observe, and where they can comment, and where they have perspective, because they sit with the people who live on the edge. So I completely endorse – and find all of that really challenging.

FRANCES: Yeah, at times I feel challenged. Challenged is the word, yeah.

And you, Carmody?

CG: I think if we're not challenged, we're not listening. It doesn't seem to me that there is a version of the gospel that isn't challenging. I think that Bernadette really puts her finger on it that 'the Church isn't called to be relevant, it's called to be prophetic'. Now, of course, the prophetic is relevant, but it's relevant because it's prophetic, it's not relevant because it's trying to fit in. I have struggled a lot with just how uncomfortable this makes me feel. On one level I don't want to be part of that community because I don't know if I can handle that. I don't know if I can live up to it. And it's *terribly* important to notice that the reason that it's good news is because every one of us is not really good enough. On some level, every one of us is broken, every one of us is weak, every one of us is fragile. And the fact that the Church is like that, as a church of the peripheries, and as a church of the excluded, is precisely what means that we can be there. It's precisely what means that, even though we're not perfect and even though we're kind of rather morally mediocre for the most part, that we have a place there. It's the fact that it's not a church for shiny people and it's not a church for the righteous and the perfect. It's exactly what makes it possible to be a member – speaking personally. But then the flip side of that is it's what requires me to then accept and work with the same logic for everybody else. That I am not to expect that the Church will not have people like me in it. People who are also confused and broken and lost. So that's where I draw the comfort from. There's the uncomfortable scale of that demand – the extreme challenge it presents to our preference for ease and sort of insulation from the world's problems. That's challenging. But it's also really good news, because it means that I have a place there too.

Thank you again. Now on to the final session, which, in the light of what we've already discussed, is a very challenging question.

SESSION 5
WHAT IS A CHRISTIAN?

Carmody, you write that 'Brother Roger of Taizé used to say that "Jesus did not come to found a religion. He came to give people life."' But a religion was founded pretty quickly, though in the earliest days of Christianity, the followers of Jesus were known as simply 'People of the Way'. You suggest dropping the word 'Christians' altogether, and instead calling ourselves 'People of the Way'. Is this realistic? I asked the Voices what they thought.

JIM: I'd be very reluctant to drop the term 'Christians'. And I think if we were to adopt the term 'People of the Way' it's subject to misinterpretation as being elitist. Being Christian is distinctive, but I don't think it is in any way elitist.

FRANCES: I often don't tell people I'm a Christian, so maybe it's a good thing to say 'People of the Way' because then people might start to say, 'Well, what do you mean?' And it might open up questions, or it might open up conversations. But certainly I can understand, or am in agreement in some ways, when she says dropping the word 'Christian' altogether. I wouldn't say, 'I am a Christian' because there are so many negative connotations that, I think, go with saying you're a Christian.

BERNADETTE: No one is going to forget that we're Christians if we call ourselves something else tomorrow. It doesn't undo all that dreadful history that we lug around with us. We are who we are. You can't unwrite the past by calling yourself something else.

Were you being serious when you suggested it?

CG: To some degree I was, I think, yeah. Surprise myself by saying that, but I think to some degree I was. Not that there should be a new policy, but that we should let ourselves really ask how we mediate our identity to those around us, and whether we're doing that in the right way. I don't for a moment think, to answer Bernadette, that this is about getting away from 'all that dreadful history we lug around with us'. We're never going to get away from that, except in so far as we can repent and heal, which, of course we're always called to do. But it's not about somehow erasing the past, it's about helping people to see that Christianity is not an '-ism'. It's not a club. It's not an association. It's not a hobby. It's not a collection of the like-minded. But it is the shared following of a person. The concept or the phrase 'People of the Way' captures that. It also captures a sense that this is not a community that's arrived. It's not a community that has a finished package. It's a community defined by a shared journey, with a shared destination, which is the fullness of joy and reconciliation in the Kingdom of God. That's what defines Christians. And Jesus didn't come to create a group of people who are all into the same thing. He came to create possibilities of life for every human being by being in his company. Christians are people who want to be part of that project. Anything we can do to communicate that to others, we should do.

Very good. thank you.

[19]
We're going to change direction a bit. I was fascinated by what Muslims are required to do when they go to the mosque to pray. They're obliged to occupy the next available space in the row that is being filled when they enter. They're not allowed to begin their own row. So social distinctions in the world outside the mosque dissolve. Why? Because before God they are all equal. That's quite an eye-opener for Christians, isn't it. Here's what Bernadette, Frances and Jim think.

BERNADETTE: I think we should be made to follow that particular rule in church and make everyone start sitting down at the front. Christian fellowship is very often about people who are like-minded, with similar backgrounds, getting together because they feel comfortable together. That's a very human thing to do. It's completely understandable. And you look at the gathering of Jesus' disciples and he's gathered a group of people who couldn't be more different from one another, but we don't tend to gather in that sort of way because we haven't got Jesus physically present with us, to help us sort out our differences. It's much easier to be with people who think like we do. Not too much challenge!

JIM: I'm not at all sure that it is like that. In the UK, the number of church buildings and the number of church communities available vastly exceeds the number of mosques, so the Muslim goes to 'the mosque' to pray; the Christian chooses which flavour of Christianity.

FRANCES: I think people tend to go and sit with their friends. So again, it is cliques really.

Have you any comments about those reactions?

CG: Christianity doesn't have the best record with social hierarchies. In many cases it's reinforced the social hierarchy – made it sacred somehow. Our seating arrangements in churches have sometimes reflected that. But that's part of the history that we've spoken about already several times, of the fact that the history of the Church is just the history of us – the history of human beings not being the best version of themselves a lot of the time. Bernadette's really put her finger on it. Christian fellowship must not be about a collection of the like-minded, because it's not based on some trivial thing that we all have in common. Christian fellowship is based on the fact that we are all one in Christ Jesus. Which is exactly what's so powerful, right, about Muslim prayer, is that when Muslims go to mosque together to pray, when they are all bowed down before God, there's no difference between them. They are all equal before God. They all perform exactly the same worship. They all prostrate themselves to the very ground, whether it's the King of Saudi Arabia or a homeless person. That's a very, very powerful witness, with the body, to the reality that they are trying to testify to, which is the universal fraternity – you know, the universal siblinghood of human beings as worshippers of the One God. There's a church that I used to go to in London, which I used to call 'the United Nations'. There were so many different ethnicities there. They all mixed indiscriminately in the pews. That was a really beautiful sign of what unrestricted fellowship looked like. Every church has the opportunity to say: 'How can we show that unrestricted community?' There are some churches where it seems to be important that you dress up to go to church – almost like there's a sort of uniform. We can make church a space in which how we present ourselves is simply not the issue. That's exactly what James is getting at, right, when he talks about how people dress when they come to church. If we can have *any* space where how you present yourself is not the issue, it should be church.

[20]
*A final question. You wrote that 'Having seen Christ, having known and
encountered Christ, the authors find themselves having to rethink the
concepts and frameworks they had received from their past, whether
Jewish or Greek.' I asked the Voices if their encounter with Christ
changed the way they think about things.*

BERNADETTE: Most days I would say that's absolutely the case,
that one is on a constant journey of engagement, and when one
is alive to that, then the way you think is always up for grabs. We
don't have to know it all. We can't know it all. So what we do
discover is all revelation. It's all brightening up and opening up of
life and potential. Yeah. Yeah. Pretty much every day something
seems to change.

FRANCES: Oh, definitely. Well, there's another scripture which
really resonates with me, where it talks about Jesus says, in
this life you will find trouble, but take heart, I've overcome the
world. So that whenever troubles come I'm reminded that we will
not be without trouble, but we will be able to overcome. And I
think my encounter with Christ has helped me through trials and
tribulations, and through life and death situations. So yes, it's
changed.

JIM: My encounter with Christ was in no sense a Damascus Road
experience. I was raised in a Christian worshipping household
and went through the usual routines of the primary Sunday
school and the senior Sunday school and regular worship. So,
has it changed the way I think about things? It has evolved. It has
evolved as life experience and understanding. I've grown, and as
I've aged it's been an encouragement really, to keep reviewing
how I am living, right to this moment.

Carmody, I guess you'll be in tune with them?

CG: Yes, I am absolutely in tune with them. It's terribly important what
Jim says. The personal identification is of some reassurance to him, he
says that there's some feelings of inadequacy. It's sort of impossible to
conceive that God has identified himself personally with each human
being, and that therefore, when I am dealing with each human being, I

am dealing with God – with Christ. It's impossible to sort of be adequate to that. To rise to that. That's a sort of an infinite goal. But the other side of that same truth is that God has identified himself personally with me – just as I am. Right now, no ifs, no buts.

In the Second Vatican Council it says: 'In the Incarnation of the Son of God, God has united himself definitively with each human being.' That's what 'incarnation' is: a union of the divine with the human. That is in some way true in each one of us. So we don't need to be afraid. The fact that it's true for everybody around us, and that I need to treat them like that, also is to be experienced in the light of the fact that it's true in me. God is already there. I don't need to prove anything. I don't need to achieve anything. I'm just a human being. That's already enough, to be united to God in some fundamental way. And that's deeply reassuring. There's nothing to be afraid of there. Yes, challenge. Yes, an invitation to something great. But nothing to be afraid of.

There's a brother at Taizé, that has a community in France, where I used to go a lot. He was asked at some point why he wanted to follow Jesus, by some friends who didn't know anything about Christianity. And he said, 'Because I wanted the adventure. Jesus promised me an adventure, and I want to go on an adventure in my life.' I think this is a really helpful way of dealing with our anxieties about Christian life. About the Christian challenge. What Jesus is calling us to is an adventure. It's not supposed to be some list of impossible moral attainments that just make us feel bad about ourselves – a little bit like when, you know, young people go on their outdoor expeditions. They know it's going to be hard. That's the whole point. They know that they're not really certain how it's going to go – that on a given day it might go well, or it might go badly, that they might get cold and hungry and tired, and lose their way, and, you know, the rain comes into their tent, and they fall into the river and all the sorts of things that happen in those expeditions. That's part of the point, right, in that you don't know what's going to happen, but you do it because it's an adventure. Because it's worth going on, because somehow you're going to grow and you're going to discover, and there's somebody there who's going to make sure that, even if you do get lost, you don't stay lost. Even if you do get wet, you don't stay wet.

Following Jesus is an adventure. It's supposed to make life more exciting and more beautiful, and more rich and more full. It's not supposed to just lay a terrible burden on your back that makes you feel like you can't get up out of bed in the morning because 'how could you ever be good enough?' That's absolutely not what it's about. Being in the company of Jesus is being with somebody who's going to go with you through all of that stuff and make sure that the journey of your life is beautiful and rich and exciting. The key extra layer of the Christian adventure, as opposed to any other adventure – and this is the whole point, in a way, that I was trying to make, in everything I said – the key point is God wants everybody to have that adventure. The condition of you having it, is that everybody else is invited. That's what distinguishes the Christian adventure. It doesn't leave anyone out. Life is supposed to be rich and beautiful and extraordinary and exciting and promising for everybody. I think that's the very best kind of adventure to be on.

Carmody, thank you so much for your responses and explanations and leading us through that adventure. There's so much more in the booklet we could enjoy discussing, but I'm afraid that time's beaten us. So my thanks go too to Jim, Frances and Bernadette, who've been our bold Voices. And thank you all who've been listening. We hope that you've enjoyed it and will enjoy using the audio, and the splendid booklet that goes with it, exploring in your groups why God has no favourites.